To . . . .

From . . . .

CATS

a guide to creature comforts

by James Croft

LAUREL
GLEN

Sleep, stretch, yawn, eat, yawn, stretch, sleep—cats lead charmed lives. But these simple pleasures conceal another life that is far from predictable—one crammed with incident, adventure, and excitement such that other animals can only dream of!

...welcome to a cat's world.

Contents

The Simple Things

Best places
to sleep:

...on the bird perch

...under the bed

...on the window sill

...in a sunny patch

...in the flowerbed

...just out of reach

Best things to eat:

...*not* cat food

...we love milk

...fresh fish

Cat Psychology

"Tell me about your childhood…"

Training has little effect.

sit, stay, roll over

Cat's chorus

Body language

happy

alert

frightened

friendly

Hunting lesson #1:

Find a good hiding place.

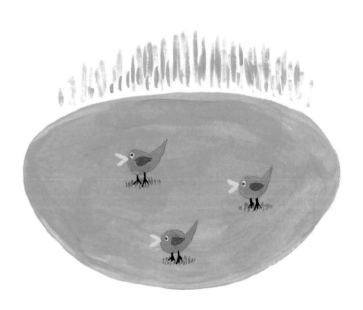

Hunting lesson #2:

Make yourself invisible.

Hunting lesson #3:

...then pounce!

Good prey are

birds

rats

fish

little pets

Bad prey...

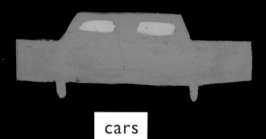

cars

televisions

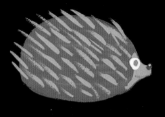

porcupines

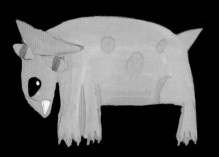

big dogs

I knew you'd be pleased.

aaargh!

Making Friends and Influencing People

Pecking order

mouse

cat

dog

human

here

Cat friends

Tiger

Bozo

Jezebel

Inky

This is where I take my special friend.

Night patrol

Playing tricks on dogs is fun.

I *do* like some dogs...

ruff
ruff

...but they can't hunt.

People are *stupid*

...a simple meow
is sometimes
not enough.

We *will* go to the fish market.
We *will* go to the fish market.

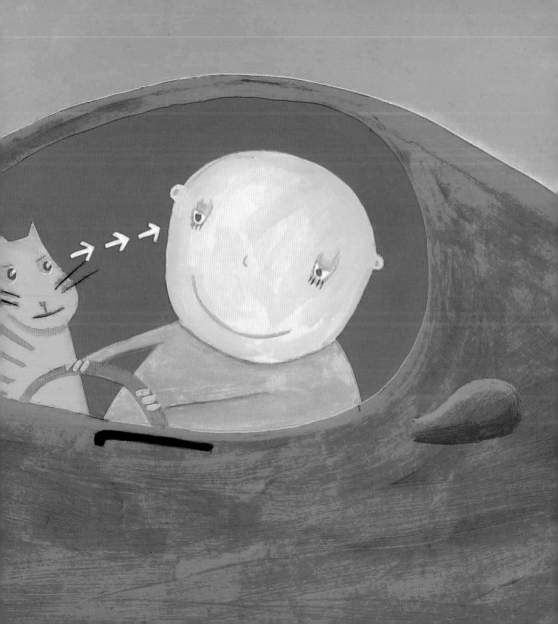

Nine Lives

Acrobat

twang!

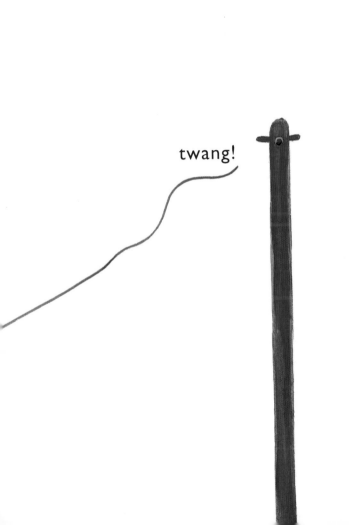

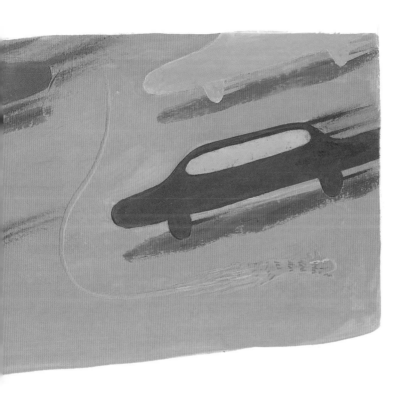

Greased lightning

Free fall

Supercool

Daredevil

"Be quiet!"

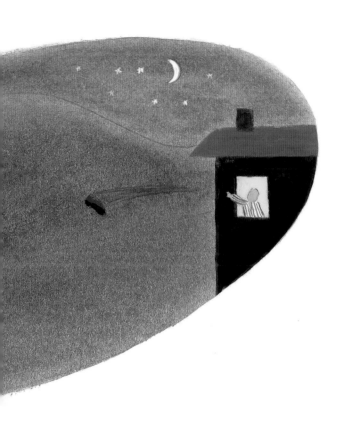

Misunderstood genius

Ninja

Sticky fingers

Run for your life!

Feline Fancies

Running with the big cats

To be waterproof

Cat burglar

Flying with the birds

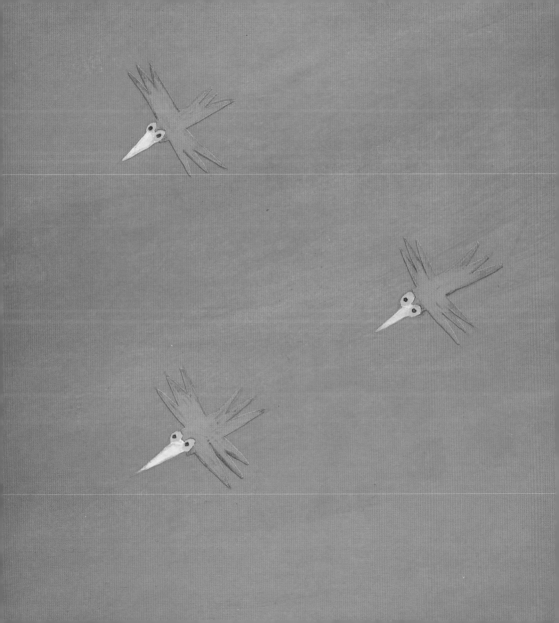

Sailing away with an owl

To be a witch's cat

"eye of newt, wing of bat"

Telekinesis: the ability
to move objects
with one's mind

To be allowed to scratch all day long

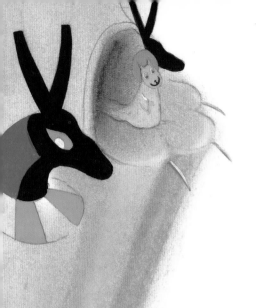

hooray!

hooray!

hooray!

To be worshipped

And behind that
inscrutable expression,
you can be sure
your cat's working on it…

About the Artist

Born in Yorkshire, James Croft studied in Cleveland, Leeds, and Wolverhampton and now lives in London. Sharing a flat with two college friends, three fish, a cactus, and numerous snails, James is frequently reminded of his rural upbringing which continues to influence his work.

First published in the United States in 2000 by
Laurel Glen Publishing
An imprint of the Advantage Publishers Group
5880 Oberlin Drive
San Diego, CA 92121-4794
www.advantagebooksonline.com

Publisher Allen Orso
Managing Editor JoAnn Padgett
Project Editor Elizabeth McNulty

Author/illustrator inquiries, and questions about permissions and rights should be
addressed to MQ Publications Ltd, 254–258 Goswell Road, London EC1V 7RL;
e-mail: mqp@btinternet.com

ISBN: 1-57145-658-9
Library of Congress Cataloging in Publication Data available upon request.

Printed in Italy

1 2 3 4 5   00 01 02 03 04